SO-BDJ-246

OWL

poems and prose by
Donald Schenker

August 10, 1930 – February 14, 1993

Press   BERKELEY, CA.

Copyright (c) 1997 estate of Donald Schenker
All rights reserved.

The following poems have appeared in the present form, or in altered forms, in the following publications:

"Album", "Empty Frame", "Nap", "The Love of Owl", "Whiff", and "Owl Contemplates Suicide" in Brief I, June 1988; "Pink" in Iowa Review, January 89; "Owl Takes Care of Himself", "Those Old Groucho-the-Owl Glasses", and "Sign" in Giants Play Well in the Drizzle, November 1988.

Cover Design by Alice Schenker
Book Design by Kalen Meyer

Published privately.
ISBN 0-9663126-0-0

Don wrote most of the poems in this book during the early months of 1988 while involved in a meditation/ visualization practice begun as a way of helping his immune system deal with prostate cancer. *Owl* was a totemic character that evolved through this process along with several other characters and a geography. (I have included a map that he once drew for me tracing the path of these daily journeys, that resulted in an image of the back of a body with organs delineated.) These visits with *Owl* quite naturally found voice in poetry but left him feeling uncertain about publishing them as a book since they were a diary of this rather unusual personal experience.

He did finally decide to put them into a manuscript which he was organizing at the end of his life. Don chose most of the poems and which version to be used before his death in February '93. I finished putting the book together with help from Tobey Hiller, John Oliver Simon, Steve Ajay, and Richard Silberg and am most grateful for their suggestions and guidance.

The following excerpted journal entry gives a description of his experience and serves as a good introduction to this manuscript.

Alice Schenker

December 26, 1991

There was always a reluctance to Owl's visits, a quality that seemed familiar to me. I needed his presence, and was deeply moved by it as by nothing in my life until then. Slowly I began to remember him, as a child recognizes that spirit in small animals. Remembering, I remembered Owl, and yet Owl seemed reluctant, almost recalcitrant. It was as if there were so many hours he had to give me; just those and no more; and that the quality of the visits was such that if I'd picked a creature more mammalian... But this *was* the quality of Owl and his visitations. He seemed to stand off and watch me as well as visit, and this caused me grief. Is this quality of distance not also the attribute of any deadly disease, and of our own selves, too? In the midst of Owl's presence was the very grief he was teaching me to feel about my own life that was slowly draining away. I was never sure whether to acknowledge this grief or deny it. Grief and abandonment. The greatest gifts brought to consciousness seem not to be enough. Life, taken for granted, never asks for more life, but the first look into the face of death implies a begging which no mere guide can answer. Owl's simple duty was to lead me through the landscape I had come from, appear to me in dreams and meditations, enter my waking hours with his fuzzy features, and remind me painfully about the unfathomable bigness of everything in which he and I were brothers more than victim and guide. It's a hard lesson I never did learn. And if I know it, like a kid in school who, in a flash of understanding, gets the problem on the blackboard, exulting, loses it on the way home. Someone says, "So what did you learn in school today?" and a flash of inkling passes through the mind and is gone.

I sat and meditated each morning, confused. I didn't want the wholesome emptiness. I wanted Owl. As if in a tantrum of abandonment, I grew more and more unfocused. Rather than focussing on my breathing, I found myself returning to scenes introduced to me in those sessions with Jay Simoneaux.* The beach. A rock pool where I was supposed to dive and come up with something, but having dived deeper than I ever thought I could go, I was propelled upward like a torpedo, a dolphin to the surface, exultant. I found myself more and more on that beach now, walking east in the afternoon to the stream which ran into the sea. Turning left, I'd follow the stream (hopping from one bank to another, perhaps) to the brush where the sand began, the vegetation, and just beyond to a small field it ran directly through. A small field or a large garden, where wheat had once grown, or corn, or vegetables, perhaps, but which was now abandoned, stagnant, flooded, smelly. I could see that there was much work to be done in this field if I wanted it to be brought back to productivity.

Still following the stream, at the end of the field was its source. The rock pool. And just beyond a small waterfall. Coming to the pool, I'd undress, dive into the cold water, letting my breath out with the momentary shock, clamber up onto the opposite side, pass through the small cascade and into a tunnel behind it (I've always called it a cave, though). Inside, the place glowed. There was no need to carry light. About twenty feet from the mouth was a turnoff to the right which I explored once to find a small room in the rock where the spirit of a prehistoric ancestor lived who had been ritually spreadeagled, tied down and flayed alive by strangers.

Another twenty feet or so was another turnoff, this one sloping down. I never took that one until months later, but always hurried through the main tunnel, always faintly lit,

---

* A Group Facilitator at the San Francisco Cancer Support Community, who helped Don begin his meditation/visualization practice.

to the summery daylight at the other end. And there was a small, amazing Beautiful Meadow.

To the left of the meadow was a great stone hill (this was the Red Hill) which hid from view the way up to its summit. That path to the top could be found only on the far side of the meadow. Once there, this walkway rose by alternating steps and steep paths to the top. It was a long climb, but it never seemed so. The view from the top of both the eastern and western sides of the Red Hill (forests to the east with water in the distance, and a steep slope down to the water just west) led me at first to think that the entire landscape was an island. Later, however, when I actually visited its extreme northern end (Owl took me there) I saw that I was on a peninsula. From the top of the Red Hill, by far the longest view was to the north, which faded away into cloudy distances. The top itself was of red clay, often blowing wildly on windy days. Very little transpired at the summit of the Red Hill on account of the wind up there, but just over the edge, on the lee (south, in this case) side was a large ledge, out of the wind, where grass grew. It was here where one day, when Owl had seemingly abandoned me, I met Nanko and his deer.

Those first weeks I felt as if Owl were suspended in a cage, over a green lawn, or park, with limited vision toward the front, and none at all behind. And the cage was fixed. As I examined this situation, I slowly discovered that the cage was Owl himself. My first feeling of his recalcitrance was that nothing was changing. Each time I checked him out, he hadn't changed. I wanted change, movement. I suggested that Owl provide benches so that we'd have a sort of park. Then children came. And the kid. And Teddy. And I had lots to do. It was clear that Owl was not there as a servant, but as a guide. His very reluctance had to suggest alternatives to my usual behavior. The powerful opacity of his back suggested my own physical past, my birth, for some reason; that Owl's back (past) was my own, and that the landscape his "back" was preventing us from seeing, was my own. Once the poem about Brother Owl was written, the cage was gone. The landscape behind us turned out to be trees. Dark ones, but trees. The entire park, in fact, with its stream running through it, receded quickly as if Owl had had me set it up only for our first meetings. Now only the stream remained.

The kid is me. Teddy is the kid's totem; what he (and I) believes is the friendly, mystic power in ourself. The kid's first appearance is on the bench waiting for the streetcar, losing Teddy. He later turns up accompanying Owl, who knocks at the door for a visit (Look Who's Here.) This poem is dedicated to Sally, a dog, who at the time was a puppy, bright and vital; didn't know any of the rules. That innocence, to me, in the midst of my experience with Owl, cancer, etc., was almost ecstatic. Letting Sally lick me, I remembered how I felt as a child. Letting down the barriers, the cages. Chopping down the dark trees.

UNKNOWN BUT SUSPECTED

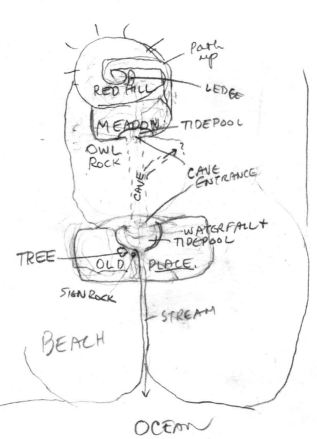

Path up

RED HILL — LEDGE

MEADOW — TIDEPOOL

OWL ROCK

CAVE

CAVE ENTRANCE

WATERFALL + TIDEPOOL

TREE — OLD PLACE.

SIGN ROCK

STREAM

BEACH

OCEAN

CONTENTS

WHO

for Jay

Handfulls of dirt stroking the glass,
say it, something out there
brushing the cloudy window of the room
empty till now,

fingers pressing on a membrane
moving the air in here,
thumping a drum of undersides, insides,

name it, a noise of feathers,
wings flexing short of flight,
whipping against skin thinning,

a window clearing, something
out there, say it, growing stronger,
say it, say what it is.

OWL, LANDSCAPER

Owl, contractor. He's
been fixing the place up
for me. It's all
so much bigger than I thought
and nowhere near
finished.

Who asked him? What does he want
for doing this?
I'm afraid to ask. One doesn't
question the likes of Owl.

He's got an office
on the very top floor. I imagine him
clawing his way through the trapdoor
here in my throat each time

just to get to his desk
day or night, whatever it takes
to make arrangements,
laying sod, curving streams,

and so far
hasn't asked for anything,
not a red cent,
not a rat's ass.

OWL TAKES CARE OF HIMSELF

Owl, preening wondrously beneath
his tight dark angles loosens

stuff that can't stand light,
dandruff stuff stuck and feeding
on the warm life under his life,

desiccated mote stuff,
flecks of trouble shriveling,
floating off forever

pissing and moaning
about the injustice of dying alone
and unregenerate.

QUESTION

Calling out for Owl, it's always
some wise guy
perched somewhere
dumb with answers.

Me.
I only wanted to ask
what are you. Were you.
Who.

A noise inside itself, like me? And who
now will make the second sound,
the meeting of eyes, the nod?

SIGN

After such silence such words
coming and going like water,
moving stones into settlement
and carrying downstream, upstream,

timestream Owl and I
talking across the creek, our words
crossing back and forth, trailing
bonds onto the third party water,
clarifying its surface, moving
stones below into understanding and witness whereupon

Owl,
used to this sort of thing, I suppose,
turns to go,
the deal struck, right?

"Wait a moment, Owl," I say.
"How about
giving me a sign of our agreement?"

Boo! he himself
is suddenly across to my side, his
wings spread, stretched out, his body like a
flag, pinion feathers straining, ribs bulging.
Some handshake, Owl!

And I spread my own arms, hands, fingers, heart
beating, beak razoring,
no end of ways to give one's word, always

one last rock clunking on the bottom.

THOSE OLD GROUCHO-THE-OWL GLASSES

Owl says
to look behind my mask
and I will find his.
Owl invites me to peek·
behind his mask and
blink! he's gone.

This is silly.
There are no such meanings
behind such words.

"Look," Owl says,
"the light you take through your eyes,
is the very light I give back through mine."

It's all so silly,
no such words behind such meanings,
really. Imagine
masks all beak and blink
hanging behind human faces hiding
owls.

THE LOVE OF OWL

Oh, I say I love Owl,
and Owl loves me,
that this is our place,

yet we meet only at the creek, that noisy spot,
demarcation that babbles by us in distractions
maybe Owl understands,
not me. Who

installed that water anyway? All I said was
there ought to be some grass here,
a burbling brook,

and there it was, the place to go,
never knowing if he'll show for sure,
if he's too busy to come when I need him,
if he knows his name, that he's Owl,

my Owl,
and when he comes, it's me
there across that sky-high water
yelling questions, hollering answers, belting out
deals, promises,
a very significant other.

EMPTY FRAME

In the downstairs full of noisy guests
no pictures of Owl.

In the dark upstairs, contemplating
the piles of empty clothes on the beds,

standing on the dressers,
taped to the mirrors,
hanging on the walls,
not a single picture of Owl.

HONOR

A brown horse with four white feet
in a blue halter in a red stall, nice
freshly painted yellow straw and green
hay all around,

and Owl, having trouble
roosting in the unsubstantial rafters,
asking me if this one 's O.K.

You call this imagery, Owl?
a brown horse on four white feet is
no death to me.
A halting blue is no mentality.
A red stall is not a heart.

We made a deal.
I asked for healing and you for honor.
"Write me a poem," you said.

Poem after poem. Image after image
of healing. I need you
thinking up better scenes than this. And this

poem, Owl,
after all the poems I've given you before,
is this O.K.?

TOWARD PREY

The feathered body, the wings
driving through a tunnel of air
toward prey

pumping so terribly clean
that direction down.

OWL, SHARK

There is a basement room where Owl
meditates,
a dark maze
of arteriosclerotic pipes and rusted angles
where Owl
visualizes (because I ask him to)

floods of light —
bright, repairing,
sweet water to the ceiling, soaking.

Seems lost
down amongst my mazes dozing,
doesn't he,
amongst such quandaries quelled? Well,

you don't know
Owl, a shark twixt
fishmice, his dazzling hide
abrading, polishing
every surface of that deep complex,
inside and out,
shining to a whiteness, with feathers and sweet water,
that place, his

dark system
whose very blood loosens (because I ask it to),
the deepest, wettest, oldest,
darkest iron.

YOU KNOW WHO

A small January owl,
perched atop the outhouse door,
watching us
move belongings into the cabin,
took a good look at
me in particular.

"Who
(the hell are
you?)"
he asked. "Ooh!"

I, eyes
wide, exclaimed
before he flapped away.

I thought it was
a January owl is all,
small, coffee-colored, big eyes,
outhouse door for a perch, whitewash
streaking down the wood under its tailfeathers, remains
of local mice, rats, squirrels. But

you know who.
"Who
(the hell are
you?)" I write again

and hide a bit of folded paper behind the beak
of a small owl escaping last winter,
gagging

until a poem, folded
and folded
and folded again,
goes down whole.

ALBUM

Owl with a big cigar, sitting
on the stoop across the street from the stationery store,
Houston & Suffolk Streets, New York, September, 1931,
with the kid on his lap.
The handles of the baby carriage lower left,
and in it is supposed to be
the teddy.

Owl with his arm around his best friend,
the two of them posing stiffly around the side
of Tepper's drug store, the Bronx, 1936.
The kid is still visible around the eyes.

Owl in the snow against the fence of P.S. 67, Winter, 1940,
wearing that wool pilot's cap he lost about that time.
The kid is still visible.

June, 1949. As a Navy pecker-checker in California,
clowning with some buddies between innings of a baseball game
Oakland Naval Hospital, Oakland, California.
The kid is still around.

San Francisco, California, 1961, A photographer,
his two children cheek to cheek on both sides of his face,
Owl shoots the three of them from arm's length
with a wide angle lens.
Three teddies simply wouldn't fit in this picture,
so they were all left out.
Note the kid in the middle.

Owl, merchant, leaning on the counter
at his grand opening, Berkeley, California, September, 1975,
with the kid in the crook of his elbow.
Note the kid in the crook of his elbow.

On the grass in front of the stream on their place,
Owl and the kid picnicking.
Note the teddy cradled in the kid's arms.
Summer, 1988, and nobody's changed a bit in all these years.

BENCHES

There are benches around the place now,
the kind from way back when on which

Owl used to set the kid down while waiting
(under one of which teddy was abandoned

forever. Oh, the kid mourned until he got another,
not the same. Owl changed, too.

Raising children.) for one thing or another,
the bus someplace, maybe. This place

getting to be a regular park, I say to Owl. Next
the bus'll stop outside, we'll have

picnics. Kids running around losing ,
people in between blades of grass. Ah,

if benches could talk, I say.
If benches could talk, says Owl,

then all that kid stuff fallen through the cracks
between their ribs waiting and dreaming

could talk back, says Owl.

BROTHER OWL

Owl and me in the womb together. Mama never
realizing the kid had turned
twin, a thing

with feathers on its back,
pinions bunched at the ends of its little arms,
feathers with spines thick as claws
curving in her soft, unconscious shell.

COMPARISON

I used to think you were small, Owl.
You used to think I was big.

Now you are my size
and I am yours.

You stretch and open and there I am,
stretching and opening to find you.

I wear you like a coat,
and you are in me like a spine.

WELL, FOR CRYING OUT LOUD, LOOK WHO'S HERE

for Jenny & Sally

The doorbell rings and here's
the kid,
a teddy under his arm big as he is, and Owl
standing there
grinning,

the three of them grinning,
and me,
Oh Me Oh My,
gathering them in,
all of us hugging and chattering away

in the foyer,
on the grass in the foyer growing,
on the sun in the foyer shining,

Owl here with the kid,
and the kid with his teddy,
all of us.

Someone ought to get a camera.

MEDICAL CENTER CAFE

Amongst the shoppes clustered
at the base of the sprawling medical center,
Owl and the kid stroll
naked in fluorescent daylight amongst
white coats, green smocks, name tags —

medicos, the waiter tells us, used to seeing
far worse than this sort of thing —
Owl-and-Kid stuff —
nude birds and naked children
waddling through doctorland holding hands,
looking for a nice place to have dessert,

the waiter seating them
at a stainless steel table on stools of stainless
steel in the deep blue shade to wait,

Owl painfully aware,
crossing his legs,
his genitals
and vent
folding over,
sitting,
the kid —

you know —
people making faces,
what's? with? that?
owl? why?
don't?
that?

kid! grow!
up! for
cris!sakes!

THE WRESTLERS

Owl and the kid
on the way home from school, dawdling,
throw their books down on the sidewalk and begin
wrestling.

Owl knows, moults in his mind to fit
between them, all three one single
instrument to joy devoted,
a cone of life
wide end up
going way, way back, and singing,
as only in such open throats can be sung,
the absolutely correct song.

OWL, WHERE ARE YOU?

Owl, is that you I hear
hooing and cooing out there in the real
Sunday Berkeley morning,

or a mourning dove?
C, B-flat, B-flat, B-flat.
C, B-flat, B-flat, B-flat.

Is it you, Owl,
or an ordinary mourning dove?

BUDDHA & THE TEA LADY

for Phil & Ginger

Owl understands
about Buddha and the Tea Lady.
Owl's in the top of the tree.

I'm down here at the bottom,
up to my ears in the stream
mixing up comings and goings, hellos and goodbyes.
One can't even hear oneself think, let alone
understand.

Buddha has a red beard and leukemia,
hair falling like platelets
in heavy gravity, ten more days
of his beautiful face (starting
a week ago Tuesday) until
nothing but blue eyes, pink cheeks, baldface.
Buddha saying goodbye to me today. And me,
can't even hear myself think, saying,
"See ya."

Ah, Owl, fill me in.

And the Tea Lady,
swollen with profound loneliness,
the chubby little hands inside her clasping
a steaming doll's cup of amniosis to her hope of health,
her child's voice drowning, unable
to swim to the telephone any more
and say hello,
goodbye,
anything at all (since yesterday, Wednesday).
See you, too, Tea Lady.

Owl, how
does one find the peace to say goodbye
when one is not the one going?

Owl?
Hello? Hello?

OWL CONTEMPLATES SUICIDE

Just the one
step off the branch,

the prey clear
at the bottom in the dark

waiting
to leap at your beak in fear

of feeding
you, insects, earth, tree,

future,
the limb where you last stood trembling

not with loss,
but with the wind,

survivor,
forever sowing sounds

of last cries once
so thrilling.

OWL, LANDSCAPER II

The office door is standing open and the shades
off the windows,
shelves emptied, walls
scrubbed.
Where are you, Owl?

Trees have been trimmed, underbrush
cleared away and burned, the smoke
dissolving the phlegm that used to coat the grass.
A bone and gristle landscape, this,
no fat in the morning mist today.

There's the smell of a sea somewhere.
The place feels suddenly

a mile higher, a thrill
of fences down, distances
waiting, ours.

Dammit, Owl,
where are you?
Come help me smell the sea.

DESCRIPTION OF THE MISSING OWL

Used to be spine, perfect, a knife
bent and serrated in a womb,
tiny fingers pinions, toes talons,
sweet baby fat sheathed
with feathers drying hard as spines.

Turned out appearing
small, soft, smooth,
color of coffee with lots of cream.
Large head. Big, dark eyes.

Grew colors — orange eyes at the vortex
of great purple circles scooped out
of a green head above a beak the white of brides,
flat black ears pointing upwards as though being shoved by
wings of a violent blue,
wings squeezing a scarlet breast to keep it from becoming
vermillion, to prevent
thighs of electric blue from igniting, burning up
legs of gold and talons of silver
from fusing with the bottoms of dreams of him.

One thing and another, got greyish.
A crown of dark feathers flaring at the cheeks.
Eyes turning shadowy. Head blackish, squaring.
Legs darkish, widening, bristling.
Feet hardening, sharpening.

Cloak over the shoulders.
Hang glider.
Carapace.

Roof on the house.
Brick wall behind a hard wooden bench facing the light.

BEHIND ONE'S BACK

Not the Owl I know,
this creature
perched along my spine
where I cannot see him.

Backbone,
jointed walking stick
that once flew.

Came down last in the dark
for prey,
great wings folded
forward over the chest.

Frozen there
in the sudden light
like ribs

encasing a new heart
half predator, half prey.
Farmer.

I KNOW YOU'RE THERE

I say Owl's up in the office.
I say he's down in the basement.
I say he's out and around on the grounds somewhere.
I say Owl's anywhere I say

and I say he's with me in this, behind me —
me saying this like this.
But you say I'm all wet.

You say
Who
the hell am am
I?
to say?
and you to listen?

What's behind these
words, anyway?
paper?
pages riffling?
high and dry?
feathers beating
under water?

Brother,
one of us is lost on land,
the other a swimmer waving
from the deepest part of the water

for help,
please

turn around so I can see you, this book
of feathers open to this page,
these very words
backwards in your golden eyes.

NAP

Flat on my back in bed,
shoes on, hands in pockets,
I dream of Owl, wingless

swimming upside down
in the sea
toward me

(high and dry,
running
upright over the waves),

amputee creatures
come great distances
to clap feet.

WHIFF

Most mornings only
traces of Owl around the place,
whiffs of his work being
forgotten in the light, fumes,
tenuous residue of that feathered

black sun filled with light, his leakings
in the grounds around me,
a drop of blood here, another
hapless mouse of cancer,

a wing-swipe on the wall downstairs,
tendon marks on the pipes showing
black instead of grey, that faint blue flush
of less dust most mornings than
the day before,
more fresh water going through today than
yesterday,

and Owl
somewhere in the dark, restless, one-eyed,
struggling for tenuous residues of the kid,
faint memories of me, the way it is.

MESSAGE

Owl takes me out to sea,
drops me in the dark water.

I thought it would hurt
to drown, be eaten by fishes,

but I'm only another message:
kerplunk, tread water, then sink.

SURPRISE

I hear the door close
soft as wings behind me as I leave.
Surprise,

Owl behind the house,
close against the back wall,
wings around the sides, touching
at the front door,
an embrace,

a hug, a squeeze, a tug
and up it comes, the whole thing

airborn, competent, Owl showing me
how real birds leave home.

SAYING GOODBYE

Glad I met you.
Glad we could get together like we did.

I shudder to think it could have been
nobody home that day. I shudder to think
of no you. Imagine,

at the end of your rope, no window
to make those desperate wingswipes at.
Imagine me not there inside in the dark.

We did well, considering.
You might have been nothing but shadow.
And I also, nothing but shadow.

THE WHITENESS OF OWL

Owl comes in white fur
to take me north.
His eyes are white, his beak, his wings,
his talons white. North
where even the sky is white.

In sky and snow we fly
deeper North. Blind, I ride
a blind Owl in whiteness becoming

ice.
Owl's wings pump until stopped
by whiteness. Us
in glass at the center of the North
at last. Now we wait.

THE SUDDEN LEAP
FROM THE KITCHEN SHELF
OF THE LITTLE WOODEN CHINESE HOUSEHOLD BUDDHA

for Phil Gammon

I am thinking of you and you fall.
In your robe and sandals, you fall.
With your beard of worn-down broomstraw you fall.
With your smiley eyes you fall.
With your hands raised in greeting you fall.

I think about you squatting on the shelf
with something to tell me, pondering
the problem of how to attract my attention.

A simple message, no rush:
there is silence in the room, in the house. Sunlight
falls through the window. Motes of dust
settle. The dishes in the dishrack show quiet
glintings of the possible. You are thinking

of me, seated, sipping tea, thinking of you without
realizing. You are watching
as I raise my head and drink tea.
I am seated in the kitchen sipping tea when

you fall. Standing up, done with your meditation,
arms stretching like an old fashioned diver, you leap.
You spend moment after moment in the air of the room falling,
planning the simple greeting you will have been calling out to me
when you strike the floor.

THE RED HILL

In the lee of the wind atop the red hill a gnarled man
in a woven robe the color of old wood stands,
five feet high on rope clog soles, holding a staff.
Epicanthic smile, muscular red cheeks,
yellow teeth and beard like white brush,
and a peculiar deer close by, nibbling the grass.

The mist about the body of the deer, the
moisture of its eyes and dark nostrils
sweet enough to drink, the wet, black muzzle
underneath, pink within — tongue, inside
of its body filled with freshness, same as mine!
The little man watching, smiling,
the fresh deer, the amazing

little brick shithouse of a man smiling,
couldn't ten full grown men knock him over if they tried,
smiling
because the deer is grazing in my body, his tears
on my cheeks, smiling, eyelids kissing,

because seeing grows that way.
Cheeks, with practice, get strong enough
to take any stroke and turn,

turn a million times smiling
because that's the way it is smack
in the center of the world, in the eye of the wind.

HEALING

for Sally

Fearless, the deer comes close.
I hug it around the neck feeling
its wonderful fur.
I open my face as it licks me
and in it goes. I admire
the delicate, tapering legs. I reach to feel
its shoulders and spine.
I run my hands over its flanks
and around below.

Hungry, I make my way in between its ribs.
I take handfulls of its entrails
and eat them. Meanwhile the deer
nibbles the fatty parts around my heart.
It tickles the walls of my veins and arteries
with its tongue. With its teeth
it chews tenderly the red muscles of my body.

Finding the tumor, he seizes it
like a coyote. Like a wolf
he throws it back to his molars for crushing.
Like a cat he purrs
breaking it down, swallowing it down as he runs

through me on all fours in my darkness,
through the short gut squeezing, passing
through the vent and out into daylight,
something on the path.

PINK

for Jack Hurth

Me with my bad back, tired, I set the kid down,
been carrying him a long way
in arms, on hips, shoulders, back, unable
to feel the joy in traveling — so heavy a bundle.

Can such a place be a destination?
Just for a minute I set him down in the dirt,
in one of the smelly furrows of this field.
I sit down myself and catch my breath.

He starts playing as if it were an ordinary place.
He throws little handfulls of it up into the air,
giggling at me to see
am I watching, do I want to play, too.
He has no idea.

Not today, kid. Just resting here a few minutes
before we go on, I tell myself.
I take his shoes off, though, his little shirt, his pants.
Naked, he prances on the bad ground.
He falls, he stands, he giggles,
claps with little clumps of it.
His little butt glows in the poor furrows.
What the hell. I get undressed myself.

If I could back off from this moment — not too far
back up the way we came, squint at this place
the way you see water in the distance
where there is none — I'd swear
there was a garden here, plenty to eat, prize
roots and greens, all with a blush to them.

THE POOR PATCH

Thanks.
Found the compost you delivered
scattered amply on both sides of the stream
ready for turning under.
Also the plow by the tree.
Went and collared the horse who'd wandered off
as far as possible from the work,
and hitched him up.

It's such a small patch, in half an hour
I dug your good stuff under with the bad.
I noticed the change to dark as I worked,
the compost wicking moisture right away.
Darker, the patch seemed even smaller,
the work easier. The hardest part
was getting that skittish animal across the creek —
rocks wavering in the bottom, I suppose.

It's going to take tons more, you know,
for which much thanks in advance.
Anything dug into that patch would help.
If nothing ever grew there again,
if there were nothing but air and light to turn under
then I would thank you for the horse and plow alone.

LANDCHANGE

for Ona and Kev

Every time I think about this place
I think of you.

Get an old truck
and a backhoe, maybe
dig all the good stuff we need,
take turns hauling it here,
dump it, turn it under,
drive back for more.

We'd take breaks and talk,
tell stories, sing songs, play the radio,
light the lanterns when it gets dark,
the kind that blaze and hiss,
drink wine.

Make a hell of a place in time.
We could do it, you know, the two of us,
day and night for as long as it takes.
It's only work.

FIRES IN THE FIELD

We were told to set fires
of rootwood
in designated portions of the field.
We did so.

No one expected it to work.
Some said so.
But we gathered the designated fuel
and set the fires.

It took more than we imagined,
finding roots
under trees nearby that could spare rootwood.
Harvesting

without damaging those trees.
Cleaning them
in the shade of those very trees using
our hands alone,

loosening nothing but the clinging soil
to be replaced
under those very trees we cut
the rootwood from.

Not to mention exactly when to set
the fires,
and exactly how. Not to mention
the prayers.

That the children were to do it
by new moon.
That into the ears of the oldest
was whispered

the manner of stacking the logs
on the ground
and where. And who of us should string
the lanterns

overhead between the trees, and how,
and how many,
and who should light them towards
that first dawn.

No one would have guessed how long
such fires would burn.
Each night, smouldering under the crops,
the rootwood.

BARRIER

The barges come loaded with crews and equipment,
with steel and manthick timbers for the purpose

of making a wall along the shore, weaving
steel amongst the trees for strength,
and pouring concrete: a dream

of keeping the sea away,
keeping creatures from crossing;
the wet separate from dry;

working, working, working
until fuel runs out, tools are lost,
machines broken down in the tangle, vessels
sunk offshore and workmen never heard from again;

flying fishes begin coming aboard over the hull,
the sea exchanging emissaries.

THE GARDEN

I know you are waiting for me,
sitting on the oaken bench by the waterfall,
patiently.

I'm not sure I will love you
as I should,
that everything you'll give me for the asking
I'll want. I'm not
like you, careless about love.

And time running out.
The bench is turning to stone.
The water is freezing.
Leaves shatter in the silence and fall
like hail, pelting
my empty outline beside you.

Too bad.
Do we both wish it were different
or is it only me?

THE OWL

Who, when the moon disappears
and the stars turn their backs,
when the house quits breathing
and hairline cracks appear on the pillow;

nights like this, with sleepers
sleeping as hard as possible; who,

when mice wait outside the doors of cats' faces,
when housepets offer their throats to wolves
when families use as little space as possible in boxcars;

who flings back bedclothes, lights lamps,
shreds curtains, pulls down shades, breaks glass
and sings at the top of his lungs?

THE SNEEZE

Owl sets down
on the nose of a stone face
in full sun,
ushers me into its dark nostrils
out of sight

for safety.
Gust after gust, Owl makes
wind with his wings to clear the dust

which settles again.
Time after time he whisks the blank eyes
and never sweeps them clear.
The rest of the day he roosts
in the crevice of the cold lips
and cannot make them speak.

In the evening, last chance, Owl
lifts, hovers, inhales,
and blows blush.
Nothing.

Inside meanwhile,
I invent fire.
I scratch upon the wall with charred sticks
pictures of Owl.
The feathery edges are done from memory,
like a sneeze.

OWL INTERRUPTED AGAIN

for Naomi Remen

Owl is at Coyote's place
playing cards with some of the others —
Fox is there, and Bear, and Eagle —
and the phone rings, and someone answers it.
"For you," he says to Owl. "Some guy named
Don Schenker." "Oh, Geez," Owl says. "Not him again."
Everybody smiles.
"Tell him I'll be there in a minute," he says,
getting up, pushing his chair back,
folding a pretty good hand. "Excuse me, fellows,
but I gotta go take care of this guy."
"Hey," Coyote says, wisecracking again, "That's life
in the Power Animal Game."

OWL AND THE ANCESTORS

No telling what Owl will do. On our way somewhere, he bucks in mid flight and shakes me loose and I fall. I realize that I'm lost. As I fall, I wonder why has Owl done this. I'll be dead when I hit the ground, and sure enough, everything breaks on impact, and I'm gone. Even the few tree limbs I crash through do not break the fall. I lie there a long time wondering where I am, taking inventory of the damage, pondering this terrible fate. Why has Owl done this to me?

After a long while, three men come by. They're not exactly men, but half-men, naked. Chattering, they begin tearing at my clothes to get them off. When I'm naked, one of them takes a leather bag of sorts, sewn with thongs and, sticking a sharp, splintered bone in the vein of my neck, holds me over the opening of this bag, so that I bleed into it. The three of them hold my legs up so that the blood will drain. They chatter and chatter.

Owl sits silently in a tree nearby, watching. It's getting dark, but these guys seem to see quite well. They're bandy-legged creatures with large heads, and very dirty. When they've drained me of blood, they turn me over on my back and, with a sharp stone, make an incision from under the point of my chin all the way down to my pelvic bone, hacking away without ceremony until I'm opened up, breaking apart my already broken ribs. These guys seem to know what they're doing. One of them expertly cuts the connections to my heart and lifts it out. Its there looking so plump in his small hand, so helpless. I feel a momentary pang while they all stop work to examine it silently. I try to talk to Owl, to ask him why he's done this to me, but I have no voice, nor does Owl seem to be listening. Then the one holding my heart suddenly thrusts it into his mouth and takes a bite out of it. It spurts blood. The others then take their turns, and soon it's gone, eaten, this heart of mine that was once, at age fourteen, suspected of having a murmur, the one in later years I ran four miles a day to strengthen, the one which beat and banged and binged and bonged for so long. My heart, whose fate might otherwise have been to lie buried in the cold ground, to rot in the dead hulk of my body in a box in the cold ground. And here's someone making a meal of it.

Silently, with their hands and faces all bloody now, sucking on their fingers from time to time to make them less slippery, they take my lungs, liver, all my internal organs. They make a pile of them. My intestines are removed by simply slicing them above the anus and below the stomach so that they can be lifted out easily, and what lovely, muted colors they are, greys, blues, and reds. None of them seems to care that I am spleen-less, that there are stainless steel staples where my spleen should be. If I told them about my operation would they care? Not at all. They pull the lymph nodes like berries from my spine, not counting them to make sure how many have been removed for my various biopsies. They take the kidneys, liver, bladder with the prostate underneath. Perhaps I should tell them about the cancer, I think, but I know they won't care. This is wonderful and amazing to me, that these creatures taking me so casually and skillfully for food couldn't care less about the tumors in my body which I so dreaded while I lived. They reach in and pull out wonders. One of them severs my genitals and separate them by hacking and tearing at the scrotal skin. He holds up my testicles. The others stop for a moment to watch as he eats one of them very deliberately. He gives the remaining one to his partners, who share it. I sigh as they take time out from their work to chew.

It's growing dark. They continue working. One of them takes a wedged stone and drives it with another stone delicately, skillfully into the top of my skull. He pries it open, splits the skull, scoops out my brain and holds it in his hands. The others stare at it for a moment in the darkening day, then sit down to eat it, pausing as before. This is the first time I am noticing how they sit. Their legs fold like newborns, solemnly, as they eat my brain. They were eager for my heart, they did their duty with my testicles, but they're no longer hungry now, when there's brain to absorb. Pieces of it fall from their faces onto their bodies, onto the ground, and they take no notice.

They've got my body cavity emptied now. All that's left is meat and bones. One of them is preparing my intestines by slicing down the entire length of them, large and small, spreading them open and scraping them clean between his hand and the stone blade. Another is making an incision around the top of both legs, just under the groin. He's peeling the skin back, down the legs, one at a time. He licks what blood is left to ooze. He peels the skin carefully all the way back down to the ankles, at which point my feet have been severed. He slides the tubes of skin down over the ankle bones, just like I've seen done with rabbits. Another of my friends is doing this to one of my arms, then the other. The trick is then to reach in, grab the narrow opening and pull, turning them right side out. They tie the bottoms of these tubes round and round with strong rafier or gut and begin stuffing slices of meat from my legs, back, ribs and arms into them. In one of the arms goes my organs, minus heart, testicles and brain. My bones are cracked open with rocks, and much of the marrow is sucked out and spit into one of the arm bags. After many of the bones have been emptied, they are unceremoniously hammered at with rocks to make as small a bulk as possible for traveling. They're going to carry me away with them.

It's getting quite dark now, and it's beginning to rain. I've lost track of Owl. He could be anywhere. Perhaps he's gone back and abandoned me. Well, I don't mind. Not now. He's put me in good hands after all, Owl has. These people deserve me. They've worked hard for me. Here they are grunting and groaning, making their way through these woods laden with me.

Many small pieces of me fall to the ground as they go. There's a fresh, hard rain now, and my blood is being washed from their bodies. I'd have hoped they'd want to have some sign of me remain on their persons, as a memento, a badge, even. They might've smeared designs on themselves with my blood, in celebration, in pride of having done such a wonderful job with my body, but they don't seem to care. They have more of me than they dreamed of possessing, and they aren't the sort to look back. I think wistfully of my orphaned shreds and bits lying in their wake. Perhaps some animals will come. I hope so.

In the dark, the sweet rain just letting up, we arrive in a clearing where tree boughs have been lashed together to form three large shelters. There are no fires. No moon, either, except for a grey-green glow in the blackness of the sky. My three seem to represent three families traveling together, a tribe. There are children, though no one is shouting, nor laughing, nor is there any sort of welcome. A short way into the clearing, the three simply drop their burden and sit down again in that curious, folding way of theirs. The others come and gather about them in the dark. The rain has stopped and the clouds are moving away. Arm and leg bags are opened and people grab and begin to eat. There are fourteen altogether, all making surprisingly little noise, seated in the wet night, chewing.

The moon shows for a moment, and there's a glint in the trees nearby. Owl. Glad to see you, Owl. Good to know that you've stayed with me. Thanks for taking me here as a gift to these ancestors. They have such small bellies, I will last for days. They will carry me with them for days.

INTERIOR SITE

This is the place where feathers from the wings of Owl
were plucked out by rats. Here is where
Long Cat died, her sex desecrated with burning sticks.
This smudge was made by Coyote growling deeply,
muzzle to rock as he died alone in the pitch black.
Up there are graven the images Tree Deer watched fade
as she choked in the mud. This crazing approximates
the voice of Ancestor Child who screamed as he died
curled and broken in a corner. See how all these marks

resemble one another, the generations without end needed
to make the cracks and flaws, the necessary pressure,
the agony required to soften stone.

OWL AND THE DARK TREE

It never seems long when Owl is taking me somewhere. Maybe if he were a hawk or an eagle, it might take longer, since those kind of birds spend more time in the sky. With Owl, I just go to the place where we usually meet and he snatches me up. He sweeps me under a wing, or maybe he'll grab me against the soft feathers of his breast to hold on, and we're off.

There are some places we've been to a few times, but you never know with Owl. He could be taking me anywhere. This particular time it's very dark, and he sets down near a tree in the middle of the woods. I have no idea where I am. The air is thick and close. It's really hard to see anything.

I ought to know better than to ask Owl why he's brought me here. He only says, "Dig a hole near the tree." I dig a hole. "Now," Owl says, "reach deep inside your body and take out all the things that are bothering you." So I reach down with my hand, and way up inside and separate all the things that seem to belong from all the things that don't, the cells that are whole from the cells that are sick. Somehow I pull on my insides with my fingers, sorting, and the rotten stuff flakes away in my hand while the good stuff remains. I put all this into the hole.

"Now bury it," Owl says, and I do.

My hands are very dirty. I wonder what to do next.

"But Owl," I say, "what if I didn't get it all?" Owl blinks.

"Dig another hole," he says, so I do.

"Now," he says, "go back in and get the rest of it."
I reach in and sure enough, I was right. There's more.
I pull it out and put it in the hole. How could I have
missed it?

Treacherous stuff. I go back in again, to make sure.
Everything seems fine, now. Clean.

"Now bury it," Owl says. And I do.

"But Owl," I say. "That was down there, where I
reached. What about the rest of me? What if it's all up
here throughout the rest of me?" He says, "Dig another
hole." And I do.

He says, "Now reach up into the rest of you," so I reach
in. I reach and sort and grab and pull, and I get out
more stuff. I show it to Owl. "More," he says. "Use both
hands," he says. So I reach with both hands, back into
my chest, my belly, my head. I finger amongst my ribs,
sorting, pulling out more stuff, and put it into the hole.
Soon I believe I may have gotten it all.

"Now bury it," Owl says. And I do.

There are three holes now which I have dug and filled
and covered over. I have reached into my body and
done a lot of work in there. I'm sore. I'm tired. I feel
nauseous. "Owl," I say. "I don't feel too well, Owl," I say.

"Dig another hole," Owl says. And I do.

"Take all those pukey feelings, those sick feelings, let
them come up, and put them in the hole." And I do.
I bend over the hole and let all that stuff go down the
hole, all the pain and all the nausea, the weakness, the
not feeling so good, all in the hole.

"Now bury them," Owl says. And I do.

I pat down the fourth hole feeling good. I'm ready to dig all night from here and back. "Owl," I say, "I feel terrific.

It's wonderful to feel well. I'm weary of pain, weakness, sickness. I'm tired to death of it."

Owl says, "Dig another hole. And I do.

He says, "Take all that weariness. Take every last sick and tired feeling, and put them in the hole." So I slip out of those feelings as I'd slip out of a dirty shirt, and put them in the hole. No problem.

"Now cover it up and pat it down," says Owl. And I do.

Except for my hands being dirty, I feel clean as the day I was born. Baby naked. And healthy. I can even see in the dark by now, I feel so good. I've done a lot tonight. "Five holes," I say to Owl. "What an accomplishment."

"Yes," Owl says. "Now dig another one."

So I dig another hole. "Owl," I say. "What's this one for?" "Just dig," he says, so I dig, the sixth. When I'm done, Owl gets into the hole. He says, "Now cover me up and pat me down."

"But Owl," I say. "Do as I say," Owl says, so I fill in the dirt on top of Owl, and pat it down and Owl's buried in the hole, the sixth hole.

What have I done? Why did Owl bring me here, and what would he do if he were in my place? I sit there in the circle of six holes around the dark tree in this dark place and I'm suddenly alone. I'm sitting on a place where, if I dug it, a seventh hole would complete the circle. "But Owl," I say in my mind. "This can't be." And in my mind I seem to hear him from deep in the earth. "Dig it," he seems to say. I dig another hole.

This time I dig the hole deep and long. I see in the dark as if it were day, the seven holes around the dark tree. In my mind I say goodbye and I get in. I hear nothing from Owl. I hear nothing from anyone. Sighing, I pull the dirt in over me and pat it all down, and I am in the seventh hole around the dark tree.

Suddenly green begins sprouting from each of the seven holes, luminous green sprouts, from the first one, the second, third and so on, all around. There are seven of them around the tree, and each of them grows thicker and reaches higher until they form a cage of thick green luminous trunks around the dark tree and over it, until there's not a man anywhere who could fit through between them, nor a bird.

And it's not so bad being there, with Owl close by, and all the rest of me. And, after all, it's not going to last forever.

OWL COMES ASHORE

for Jim LeCuyer

Just after dawn, someone approaches the coast
in a feathered boat,
a boy, naked but for a feathered mask.
No one waits for him.

One day there will be songs about this,
the water slapping, the breathing inside the mask.
There will be dances,
prow jutting breast, paddle arcing wings.

Then there will be nothing.
Later, there will be neither singing nor dancing,
and not too long after that, vegetation will grow
clear down to the coast like feathers.

DONALD SCHENKER

Born in Brooklyn, New York, 1930. Grew up in the Bronx.
Joined the Navy after High School and was stationed in
California. Discharged in 1949. Studied art and architec-
ture at Cooper Union, New York. Painted. Married and
moved to San Francisco in the '50's and was active in the
literary scene of that place and time. Opened a picture
framing shop in Berkeley in 1965 in partnership with his
wife, selling art reproductions and posters, later publish-
ing posters and underground comix. Sold the business in
1985. Diagnosed with cancer that year.

Has published four volumes of poems: POEMS (with
David Meltzer,) privately printed, San Francisco, 1957;
SAY X, Print Mint, Berkeley, 1971; UP HERE, Ahsahta
Press, Boise, 1988; HIGH TIME, Clear Mountain Press,
Oakland, 1991; as well as work in numerous magazines.

Died in February, 1993.

CALIFORNIA COLLEGE OF ARTS & CRAFTS

I CAC 00 0081209 T

PS
3569
.C483
O9
1997

DATE DUE